Table of Contents

From Land to Water 4

Life Cycle of a Turtle 22

Picture Glossary 23

Index 24

To Learn More 24

From Land to Water

A turtle comes on land.

She digs a hole.

Why?

It is her nest.

nest

egg

She lays eggs in the nest.

She buries them.

Then she goes
back to the water.

A few months go by.
The eggs crack!
Hatchlings break out of the shells.

hatchling

They dig out of the nest.

They crawl to the water!

juvenile

After a year,
they are juveniles.

They eat bugs
and plants.

They grow big.

Some turtles live in lakes.

Others live in the ocean.

15

Years go by.

Now they are adults!

They swim back to
where they were born.

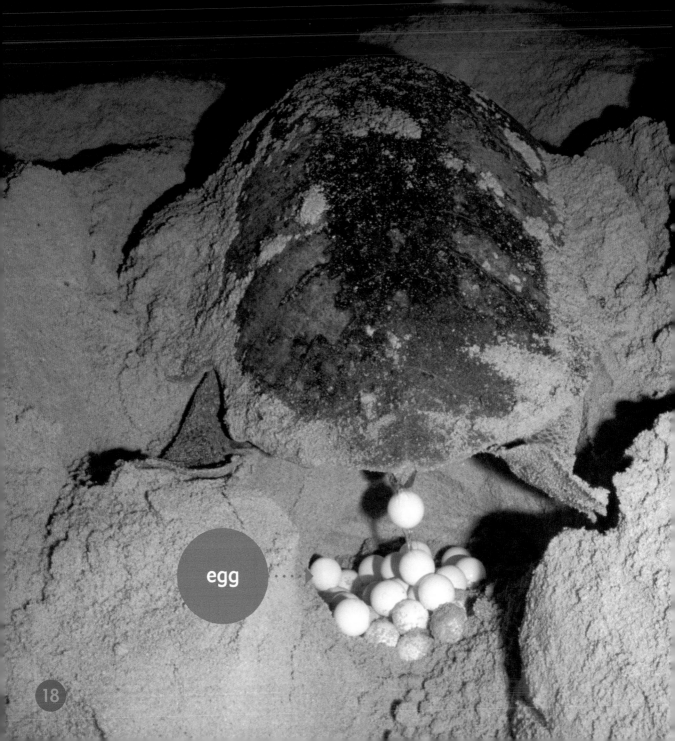

egg

This one digs a nest.
She lays eggs.
The life cycle
starts again.

Hatchlings break out.
They crawl to the water!

Life Cycle of a Turtle

A turtle's life cycle has four stages. Take a look!

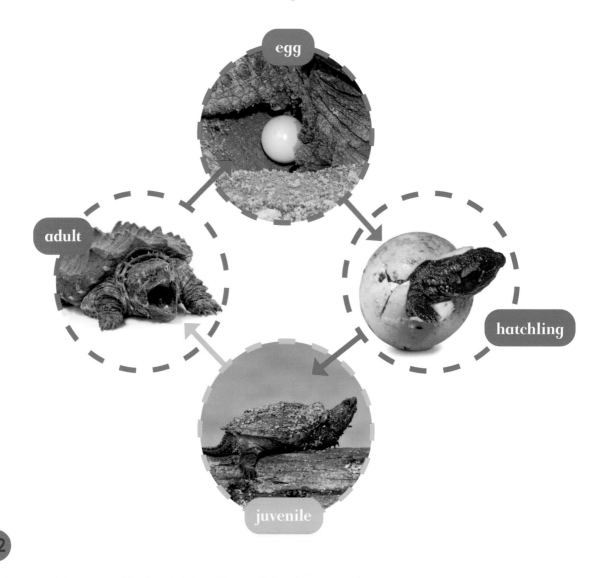

egg

adult

hatchling

juvenile

Picture Glossary

buries
Hides something underground.

crack
To break or split without completely separating.

crawl
To move slowly on short legs.

hatchlings
Young turtles that have recently hatched from their eggs.

juveniles
Young turtles in the stage of growth between hatchlings and adults.

life cycle
The series of changes each living thing goes through from birth to death.

Index

adults 16

crawl 10, 20

digs 5, 9, 19

eat 13

eggs 7, 8, 19

hatchlings 8, 20

juveniles 13

lakes 14

nest 5, 7, 9, 19

ocean 15

swim 16

water 7, 10, 20

To Learn More

FACT SURFER

Finding more information is as easy as 1, 2, 3.

❶ Go to www.factsurfer.com

❷ Enter "aturtle'slifecycle" into the search box.

❸ Choose your book to see a list of websites.